stitch divas

charlotte liddle & rachel henderson

stitch divas

...girls get creative with yarns & threads...

Coats
Crafts UK

Where ideas live

A Coats publication

First published in 2008 by Coats Crafts UK
Lingfield Point
McMullen Road
Darlington
DL1 1YJ

Copyright © 2008 Coats Crafts UK

Project editor Susan Berry
Art editor Nicky Downes
Designer Ama Amponsah
Proof reader Katie Hardwicke
Photography Charlotte Liddle and Rachel Henderson
Line illustrations Ama Amponsah
Fairy illustrations Michelle Clitherow

British Library Cataloguing in Publication Data
A catalogue record of this book is available from the
British Library.

ISBN 978-1-906007-55-3
Reproduced in Singapore
Printed in China

Contents

Charlotte

Rachel

Introduction.

Charlotte and Rachel are the new "stitch divas" of the textile world. They love stitching and making crafty things, especially with their friends. To spread their love for all things crafty, they have joined together to inspire all the young girls and their friends around the world who might like to become stitch divas themselves.

Their book is filled with quick-and-easy funky projects that show you how to make stylish things like bag charms, shoe decorations, felted jewellery, stitched purses, bangles and gorgeous cosies for your ipod or phone using a range of craft techniques, such as very simple knitting, crochet, felting, sewing and embroidery. The projects will introduce you and your friends to both traditional and modern textile crafts.

Charlotte and Rachel believe that the best way of making things is to do so with your friends. Working with other people is so much fun and will give you the confidence to learn new skills, experiment with techniques and come up with your own project ideas. Why not pick up your stitching kit and start a new trend by crafting at school, at Brownies or Guides, at clubs or even during break-time in the school playground?

If you would like to become a designer or maker, then this book is the perfect place to start. It's jam packed with fantastic ideas showing you how you can work alongside your friends to set up craft fairs and stitch clubs.

Hello, my name is...

Charlotte.

I'm 25 years old and I live in a very "vintagey" and pink house in Darlington in the north-east of England.

Let me tell you a bit about myself...

As a young girl I was always into crafts and loved spending time making things. I was a dancer until I was 15, so I spent many years surrounded by sparkly colourful costumes (I think this may be where my love for beads and sequins comes from!). Art was my favourite subject at secondary school so when I left I decided to study fashion and textiles at college and then eventually went on to do a degree in Textile Crafts at university in Huddersfield, West Yorkshire.

I set up my own business when I left university and started working as a freelance textile designer and maker. I began by working with Coats Crafts UK on projects and ideas for their website, as well as demonstrating their many products at shows like the Knitting and Stitching Show.

I also make very colourful clothes, accessories and ballet shoes which are sold in a number of different ways. Sometimes I sell them as designs to big companies, which then put them into mass production. They are also sold to individual people through my website and at shows.

Some other things I've been up to...

My first book *Stitch and Sparkle* was written and published by Coats Crafts UK in 2007. Like this book it is very lively and full of exciting projects. I'm passionate about textiles and love teaching people how to make new things.

I run workshops in schools and community centres and now have my own stitch group based in Darlington.

Hello, my name is...

Rachel.

I'm 27 years old and I live in my very woolly and colourful flat here in Edinburgh in Scotland.

Let me tell you a bit about myself...

I've always been very creative so when I left school I went to art college in Aberdeen, in the north of Scotland, where I studied Textile Design and Surface Decoration.

I realized when I was at art college that I really liked making and designing things using hand craft techniques such as knitting, crocheting and felt-making, so after I left I started to make and sell my own designs which I sold in shops and through events and exhibitions I set up with my friends. At the same time as this, I started working for Coats Crafts UK, for whom I ran workshops on knitting and crochet at department stores all over Britain.

In the last few years I have started up my own knitting club – to try and bring together other creative people in Edinburgh – which I still run.

Some other things I've been up to...

I have written three books – *Pub Knitting*, *I Love Knitting* and *I Love Crochet*. This has been really exciting as I have been able to inspire, and share my ideas with, people all over the world and teach them new skills.

Over the years I have featured in a lot of magazines and newspapers, and on radio stations and even on the news, which has been really good fun!

I really like teaching which is something I do a lot these days. I run a variety of craft and textile workshops for young girls and boys at various primary and secondary schools in Scotland.

Stylish
Cool...!
Glamerous

Getting started.

There are lots of great projects in this book for you to have a go at but it would be helpful to have some basic bits and pieces before you get started. The tools and materials shown here are not all essential for every project, but they are all used in the book. As you collect the different items, it is a good idea to keep them in a little work bag or box, so you can find them easily when the urge to be creative comes over you.

Beg or buy a good pair of dressmaking scissors, but don't use them for cutting paper, as it will blunt them and make cutting fabrics more difficult. Once you have taken needles and pins out of their packets, it is a good idea to keep them pinned to a little piece of surplus felt, so you can find them easily.

Some of the techniques for projects need some special equipment, such as knitting dollies for French knitting, for example. You will find details on page 94.

Bondaweb

Useful for sticking fabrics together.

Crochet hooks

You will need a couple of crochet hooks in different sizes for the crochet projects in this book.

Tape measure

Keep one handy. It is often useful for checking measurements.

Scissors

You will need some sharp scissors, such as a pair of dressmaking shears (for cutting fabrics) and small embroidery scissors (for cutting threads).

Buttons and beads

Keep a selection in your workbox.

Needles and pins

Keep needles and pins on a spare piece of felt when not in use. You will need both fine needles (sharps) for fine threads and thicker needles for wool yarns.

Yarns and threads

Anchor Tapisserie Wool
Good for embroidery or for finger knitting or crochet.

Coats Cotton sewing thread
Useful for stitching on buttons and beads, and for sewing up.

Anchor Pearl Cotton
Embroidery thread like this is great for decorative hand stitches.

Felting yarns

You can use pure wool yarns for knitting, crochet, and felting and special wool tops (like Anchor Filz-it) for felting.

Hand and embroidery stitches

Learning to stitch by hand is like any other skill: practice makes perfect. You will need to be able to use a needle and thread for several of the projects in this book, and some require a little basic hand embroidery, too.

None of the embroidery stitches are difficult to learn, but if you practise on a scrap of fabric first, your stitches will be neater and more professional-looking. You can work your stitches in fine embroidery threads for a delicate effect or in much thicker wool yarns for a more dramatic impact.

You will need an embroidery needle with an eye large enough for the thread or yarn you want to use. The threads you choose can make a considerable difference to the results. Thick, fat yarns will result in a chunky, naïve effect. Embroidery silks will have a much smoother, more delicate appearance.

Running stitch

This is the simplest embroidery stitch, known as a straight stitch. You simply work from right to left (if right-handed) and, working with a thread knotted at one end, you pass the needle and thread in and out of the fabric in a line, taking two or three stitches onto the needle before pulling the needle and thread through the fabric. You can use the stitch to gather up fabric, too. (A)

Chain stitch

This popular stitch can be used to outline motifs. To work the stitches, take the needle through the fabric on the right side and bring it up again to the right side a short distance away, looping the yarn around the needle in a small circle before making the stitch. (B)

Lazy daisy

This is a variation on the chain stitch and, as the name implies, it makes a pretty daisylike design. Basically work a normal chain stitch, but then take a further small securing stitch at the tip of each chain. Work five stitches in a circle to make a little daisylike flower. (C)

Seed stitch

Seed stitch is so called because it looks like seeds scattered on the ground. It is made with a series of tiny stitches that can face in different directions, to produce a random effect. It can be used to fill areas with colour to create a sparkly effect. (D)

A
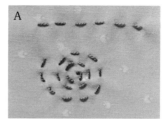

B
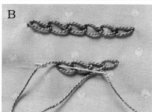

C

D
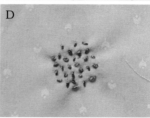

E

F
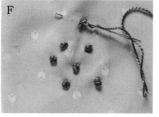

Cross stitch

A geometric stitch in the straight stitch family, this is one of the most popular embroidery stitches in part because if you work it on an open-weave fabric, you can create very neat little rows of stitches. I prefer a more freehand version, and find the irregularity adds to the charm. Work one part of the diagonal cross (from bottom right to top left) and then take the needle and thread behind the work to create the opposite-diagonal that crosses it. Continue along the line in this way. (E)

French knots

These are raised stitches formed into little knots by winding the thread around the needle three or four times in the course of making the stitch, so that each stitch resembles a small bead. It can be hard to create evenly formed knots, so practise first on a piece of spare fabric if you want a professional-looking finish. (F)

Machine stitching

You need to be able to use a sewing machine for a couple of the projects in this book. Sewing machines vary so it is important to refer to the manual for specific instructions. Your machine will allow you to choose stitch types and stitch lengths.

Two fairly simple stitches are useful: straight stitch (which creates a single line of stitches) and zigzag stitch (which as the name implies, forms a zigzag line of stitches).

Seams are stitched using straight stitch. To stitch them on medium-weight cotton with standard cotton thread, set your machine to straight stitch and adjust the stitch length to around 2.5.

For decorative stitching or for neatening edges or seams, you can use zigzag stitch. Again, for standard weight cottons, set your machine to zigzag stitch and use a stitch length of 2.5 for a basic zigzag.

To stitch a seam

Place the fabric to be stitched right sides together. If the pieces are small, you don't need to pin them, but longer seams will need to be pinned first (at right angles to the stitching line). Straight stitch parallel to the edge, roughly 1cm (½in) from it, to allow for the fabric fraying. Neaten the frayed edges with zigzag stitch if you wish.

To make a simple bag shape

Place two rectangles of fabric cut to the size required, right sides facing. Stitch around the edges, leaving a 1cm (½in) allowance all around. Turn the shape inside out and finish off the raw edge by folding the right side to the wrong side and stitch it in place.

Free-motion embroidery

Free-motion embroidery allows you to machine stitch in random patterns. It uses a special attachment called a darning foot, which allows you to move the fabric in all directions while stitching. To do this you need to use a darning foot attachment and disengage the clamps (feed dogs) on your machine which keep the fabric in place. You can work different stitches using free-motion embroidery, but basic stitches such as straight (A) or zigag (B) in this book are all you will need. You can form circles or coils (C) by moving the fabric in a circular motion.

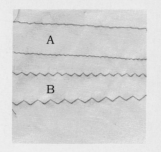

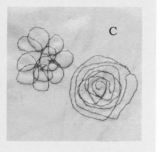

Free-motion outlines

Free-motion embroidery outlines are a quick way to embellish patterned fabric. You can add highlights to areas of your fabric by simply machining around the shapes and patterns. Use a contrasting colour or sparkly thread to get the most impact.

Free-motion quilting

Free-motion stitching can be useful when you want to attach layers of fabric together (known as quilting), with wadding sandwiched between the layers. You can stitch them together using the patterns on the fabric as a stitching guide: this is a lovely technique for adding interesting textures to the surface of the fabric.

Charlotte says:

Adding sparkle is an embellishment: this word means to make something more decorative, elegant or noticeable.

Adding sparkle

You can do this in various ways by adding rhinestones, beads and sequins. The choice of decoration and the way in which you apply it will depend on the effect you want – casual or smart.

Iron-on rhinestones

Iron–on rhinestones are a great invention! They are so quick and easy to use and produce stunning effects. They come in a range of designs but can often look more effective when cut into segments and re-placed onto fabric. Simply peel off the backing paper and place the motif face down onto fabric. The motifs are slightly sticky so they will stay in place as you iron the backs. Turn the fabric over and apply heat, using an iron, for a few minutes in order to melt the glue on the rhinestones. Peel back the top plastic to reveal a stunning rhinestone embellishment.

Beads and sequins

Beads can be attached to decorate fabrics. Why not combine them with rhinestones and hand stitch for an interesting surface pattern? Beads or sequins can look fantastic in the centre of florals and can really lift and enhance a pattern. Stitch beads close together for intense decoration or just add one here and there for a more delicate effect. Or use them to enhance a simple geometric pattern, such as stripes or checks.

Appliqué

Appliqué is a great technique for combining pattern on pattern. It's perfect for adding floral, patterned and printed fabrics as an embellishment to denim or plain fabric. Fabrics can be appliquéd very easily by glueing them using fusible sprays and Bondaweb, or you can stitch them on using hand or machine stitches. Use whatever method you prefer.

Machine stitch appliqué

Simply cut out shapes from patterned fabric and pin onto plain fabric. For circles or intricate shapes, use the darning foot on your sewing machine and free-motion stitch around the shapes to secure them in place. To avoid fabric moving around, secure it with Bondaweb (right) before machine stitching.

Hand appliqué

Cut shapes from patterned, printed or floral fabric and pin onto ground fabric. Hand stitch around the shapes. To vary the design use different decorative stitches such as Chain stitch, Running stitch or French knots (see pages 14–15). Again, to prevent the appliqué fabric moving as you stitch, use Bondaweb.

Bondaweb appliqué

Bondaweb is used to fuse two fabrics together. Cut out two similar sized squares, one from your chosen appliqué fabric and one from the Bondaweb. Place the Bondaweb, rough side down, onto the back of the square of fabric and use an iron to melt the glue. The Bondaweb is now stuck to the fabric, so you can cut out shapes or around florals. Peel the backing paper from fabric; place the appliqué shape onto your chosen plain fabric and iron again to fuse both fabrics together.

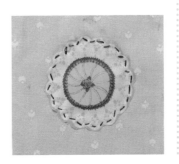

Rachel says:

There are different forms of felt – you can make flat sheets or 3D balls. To learn the basics follow my steps here.

Your most important piece of equipment when you felt is bubble wrap. This helps agitate the piece of fabric you are working with and transforms it into felt. You can choose whatever colour of Anchor Filz-it wool tops that you like best.

Felting

There are two stylish jewellery projects in this book for you to try with your friends and they are made using basic felting. Felting is such a cool technique – all you are doing is agitating wool with soapy liquid, which makes the wool fibres bind together and reduce in size, so it becomes thick and flat – it's almost like magic! By simply using some special Anchor Filz-it wool tops, soapy liquid, bubble wrap and your hands, you can create a fabric from which all kinds of designs can be made.

Just follow my simple steps and try out the different ways of creating felt and then have a bash at the project ideas on pages 36 and 60. Remember – you don't need to stick to my guidelines, you can change colours, shapes and materials as you wish.

You will need:

Detergent (or Turbo
　Filzer solution)
Glass tumbler
Water sprayer
Sheet of bubble
　wrap
Sheet of plastic
Anchor Filz-it wool
　tops
Teaspoon
Bamboo mat
Towel

1. Make your felting solution by adding a couple of drops of detergent to a glass filled with hot water and to a water sprayer. Put your sheet of bubble wrap on a waterproof surface.

2. Take some wool tops and pull them into tufts with your fingers. Start to make layers, laying the tufts of wool on top of each other, first in one direction in one layer, in the other direction in the next layer, and so on. The more layers, the firmer and stronger your felt will be.

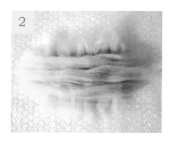

3. Using your water sprayer, spray some diluted detergent on both sides of the fabric and then, using a teaspoon, sprinkle some of the detergent mix on top of the fabric, press down onto the fabric.

4. Using your fingers, agitate the wool in a circular motion so that the fibres all start to bind together. Keep turning the fabric over, making sure you are agitating both sides of it. Sprinkle on more detergent solution if needed, as it is rubbing and wetting the wool that causes it to felt.

5. To make your felt stronger and thicker, place some bubble wrap on top of it as well as underneath it and rub well with the bottom part of your palm or with a rolling pin. Remember to keep turning the felt over and working on both sides.

6. To make the felt even stronger, roll it backwards and forwards in a bamboo mat several times (known as fulling).

7. Now get rid of the excess soapy water by rolling the felt in a towel.

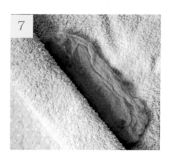

The techniques I show you on the next few pages – finger knitting, crocheting and French knitting – all make textiles with wool yarn using continuous stitches. For finger knitting you need only the yarn and your hands. Crochet needs a crochet hook and French knitting a little spool with a hole in the centre and pins around the top. They are all very easy to do.

Finger Knitting

Here is your chance to find out how to finger knit. Finger knitting is such a cool technique and it's really simple to master. Your fingers are the only equipment you need; they are like knitting needles but make less noise! You don't need anything else apart from a ball of wool.

You can finger knit by yourself or with a friend. The great thing about finger knitting is that it's really portable. You can do it on the way to school, on the bus, train, car or on the plane when going on your hols!

You will need:

Your fingers
Ball of Patons yarn
Scissors

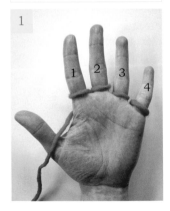

Casting on

1. You need to cast on your stitches with your ball of wool. Using your left hand if you are right-handed (and vice versa), turn your hand over, palm facing you, and let the tail end of the wool hang down across your thumb. Working with the ball end of the yarn, loop the yarn around each finger in turn (except your thumb) starting with finger 1 (make sure there is only one loop on each finger facing you and no crossed over bits!).

Your first rows

2. Once you have made a loop on each finger, take the ball end of the yarn back across your fingers (from 4 to 1) as shown and make sure the yarn is lying above each loop on your finger.

3. Now, pick up the loops around each finger one by one with the other hand, taking each loop up and over the yarn lying above it so you make a new loop on each finger in turn (but only one loop at a time). This is Row 1 of your knitting.

4. To make Row 2, start from the side you made your last loop and repeat Step 3. (Remember to make sure your yarn is lying above each of the loops on your fingers.)

5. Repeat Steps 3 and 4 until you have created the length of finger knitting you require. If you turn your hand over you will be able to see how your knitting is progressing.

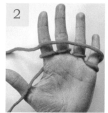

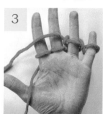

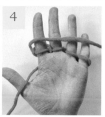

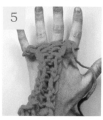

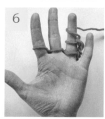

Casting off

6. When you want to stop knitting, do not lay the yarn across your fingers again. Each finger should have only one loop on it. Lift the loop off finger 4 onto finger 3. Carry the ball end of the yarn around finger 3 (anti-clockwise), lift the loop lying below the yarn up and over it and off the finger as if you are knitting it.

7. You will now have two loops on finger 3. Lift the bottom loop on finger 3 up and over the top loop. Now take the loop left on finger 3 and place on finger 2 and repeat as for finger 3. On the last finger remove the remaining loop, cut the yarn and pull the yarn through the loop to fasten.

Rachel's tip:

If you want to knit just using three fingers follow the steps above but make the loops around only those fingers you would like to use and carry the wool across in the same way.

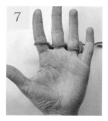

Crocheting

Here is your lesson on crocheting. This technique is very simple, but it does require a little practice to be able to make nice even stitches.

If you use it with French knitting, you can make my bag charm projects on pages 46–50. It also enables you to make little strings for attaching flowers or charms, or for bows.

To make crochet stitches, you need a medium-sized hook and some suitable yarn, but you can crochet with anything flexible including ribbon or wire. To make my projects in this book I used Patons yarn and a size 5 crochet hook.

You will need

Ball of Patons yarn
Crochet hook
(medium size)

Rachel says:

First steps to crocheting

Crocheting is a great way of making fabrics. In this book I show you how, by using a hook and some yarn, you can make simple chains to turn into flower shapes (see page 48) or a scarf (page 71). For these you need only the basics of crochet. These are:

1. How to make a slip knot.
2. How to hold hook and yarn.
3. Making your chain stitches.
4. Making a slip stitch.

Making a slip knot

1. Lay the tail end of the yarn on a table, and create a circular shape by crossing it with the ball end of the yarn.

2. Pull the ball yarn up through the letter '0' to form a loop, as shown. Pull the loop tight and place it on your crochet hook.

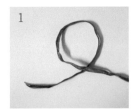

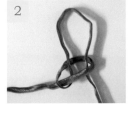

Holding hook & yarn

1. Hold the hook in your right hand (like a pencil) and hold the working yarn in your other hand.

2. Wrap the yarn around the other hand, with the working yarn under the third and fourth finger and over your first and second. Hold the slip knot in your left hand as shown.

Making a chain

Lift your yarn finger up and push the crochet hook under and over the yarn, catching the yarn with the tip of the hook. Pull the hook and yarn through the slip knot on your hook. This is your first chain stitch. Now make as many as you need.

Slip stitch

This stitch is useful for joining chains of crochet. Make a row of chain stitches (to the length needed).

1. Push the crochet hook into the chain stitch from front to back and, taking the hook under the working yarn, catch the yarn with the tip of the hook.

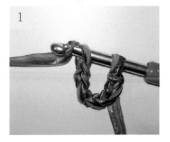

2. Pull the hook and yarn right through the chain. You should always only have one loop on your hook.

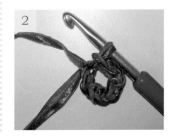

Rachel says:

French knitting is really great for any project that needs a length of tubular knitting. The size of the French knitting spool and the number of pins on it will determine how thick your tubular knitting is. The length depends on how many times you work around the pins on the spool. With tubes of French knitting you can make bag handles, coiled flowers or even little coasters if you wish. Why not try to think of lots of different things you could make from a long length of French knitting?

French Knitting

French knitting is similar to knitting on your fingers (page 22) but a round spool with pins around the edge and a hole in the centre through which the stitches you make are fed, takes the place of your fingers. Because the spool is round, so is your knitting: you create a neat little tube of knitting.

You do not have rows as such in French knitting – you just keep making stitches as you work around the pins on top of the spool. There are different kinds of French knitting spools. The simplest can be a cotton reel with some nails in the top. The one used here is a bit more sophisticated. It comes in various sizes, which will determine the thickness of your tube of knitting.

You Will need:

Patons yarn (or yarn or thread of your choice)
Prym French knitter with pick

Casting on

1. Put the tail end of your ball of yarn through the French knitter tube so that it hangs below it. Make a slip knot (see page 25) and place it onto the first peg. Now wrap the yarn around each of the other pegs clockwise in turn so that there is a single loop facing the front of each pair of pegs. Do not wrap the yarn too tightly as otherwise you will have difficulty moving it over the pegs in Step 2.

Your first rows

2. Once you have wrapped the yarn around each pair of pins, you can start to knit. Lay the working yarn in front of the first pair of pegs, and using your pick, lift the wrapped yarn on the first peg over the working yarn.

3. Continue going around and around until you have created a long tube.

Casting off

4. To cast off, lift one loop off one peg onto the one beside it, take the working yarn across this peg, lift the middle loop up over and off the peg and then the bottom one up over and off. Move this loop onto the next peg now. Do the same with the rest until you have just one loop left. Cut the working yarn and thread it through the last loop.

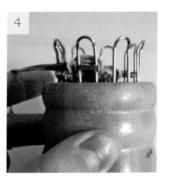

Flowery shoes.

Do you own a pair of boring pumps, trainers or flip-flops? Are they calling out for some funky decoration? Why not try this project which uses a flower loom to create cool little flowers that can be embellished and glued to your shoes for a unique look?

Charlotte says:

Making flowers is easy with a flower loom. It comes with a selection of pegs that can be put into different holes to make small or large flowers. The first time, make a big flower to practise, putting the pegs in the outermost holes. Once you can make nice large flowers, move the pegs and start making smaller flowers. Make lots of different flowers using ribbons, yarn, string or whatever takes your fancy!

Making flowers

The possibilities are endless – the basic instructions are shown below but once you've got the hang of it try using braids, ribbons, strips of fabric, yarns and even threaded sequins to make the flowers. Layering up flowers can look really effective, especially if each one is made in a different colour and material.

With a little imagination and a delve into your button and bead collection, these flowers can be embellished in so many different ways to match the colours of your shoes or to create something more wacky and contrasting. Play, play and play some more!

Using a flower loom

1. Put the pegs in the flower loom. Push one end of ribbon down through the centre opening; hold the end. Start to work a figure-of-eight shape around a pair of opposite pegs.

2. Once you have completed your first figure of eight, catch the ribbon on the last peg and continue to work your next figure of eight, making sure you work the ribbon around the last peg so that eventually the ribbons will overlap on each peg.

3. When you have covered each peg, thread a needle onto the loose end of ribbon. Bring it across to the opposite side of the flower and push downwards through a gap until it comes through to the underside.

4. Turn the flower loom over and tie both loose ends together in a knot as tight as possible.

Stitching the flower

5. Now secure the figures of eight by stitching them together at the centre of the flower. Thread a needle with a strong hand sewing thread (Stranded Cotton is fine), and stitch across the centre of all the figures of eight in a star shape.

6. Turn the flower loom over and, as before, tie the loose ends of thread in a tight knot. Now gently pull the flower upwards and off the pegs. Trim any long bits of ribbon and thread from the back of the flower.

Finishing off

7. Make three flowers, one large and two small, put them on top of each other, and stitch through all the layers (using a button).

Applying flowers

You can add the flowers to shoes or trainers, as you wish. Add matching flowers to a pair of pumps, or add a couple of flowers to the sides of a pair of funky trainers. You can also use the flowers in other ways: for example to decorate a bracelet (page 38) or on a bag or purse (page 45).

Felted jewellery.

Would you like to have a go at making your very own jewellery? It's great fun and very easy to do. You just need an Anchor Filz-it felting kit (or pure wool tops). It takes almost no time to do, and you can then decorate your rings or bracelets in different ways to give them your own personal touch.

You will need:

Flat felt (pages 20–21)
Anchor Filz-it wool tops
Piece of card
Anchor glitter felt
Bondaweb
Beads and sequins
Sewing pins; needle
Coats Cotton sewing thread
Brooch pin

Funky felted ring and brooch

I made the matching ring and brooch design shown opposite by making flat Filz-it felt (which I showed you how to make on pages 20–21). I decided to use a butterfly shape and decorated my final designs using Anchor Style & Filz-it ready-made felt, sequins and beads.

By experimenting with Filz-it colours, different kinds of ready-made felts and embellishing techniques, you can create all kinds of funky ring and brooch designs.

Making the felt base

1. Make a flat piece of felt. To jazz up your felt you might like to add different colours of Anchor Filz-it wools, threads or even sequins like those I have used in my brooch design. If you are doing this, make sure that you lay a thin layer of Filz-it wool tops over the added-in embellishments, spray over the top of the fabric with some diluted detergent and agitate again using bubble wrap before drying the fabric.

2. Once your felt is dry you can cut out your required shape. If you are making a felt ring, measure round your ring finger first, and then cut the felt a little longer, so the ends overlap. Stick or stitch the ends together.

Making the butterfly design

You can make a little butterfly ring or brooch, for which you will need to make a template from a butterfly design, such as the one on page 44. You can decorate it with buttons, beads and sequins.

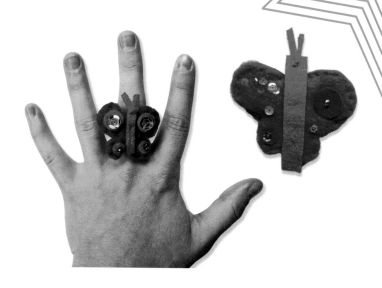

1. For your butterfly design, you need to cut out your required butterfly shape, having first transferred your butterfly shape onto a piece of thin white card. Check the measurements and then make your felt a little bigger all around than your template.

2. Once you have your required shape, cut out a similar shape in Anchor felt to act as a base. Bond the two pieces of felt with Bondaweb (page 19). To decorate your final design you might like to use beads, sequins and ready-made felts.

3. Finish off the brooch design by attaching a brooch pin to the back of your brooch fabrics. Finish off the ring design by attaching your butterfly to your cut-out felt band (made in Step 2).

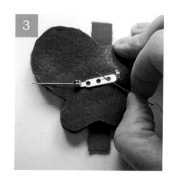

It is up to you how many balls you make to create your bracelet, the amount will depend on the size you make them. Remember not to make too many, otherwise your bracelet might be too big for your wrist! Perhaps you could make a necklace to match your bracelet and make lots and lots of balls, some big and some small. Just experiment and have fun!

Why not work together with your friends and try and create your own felted ball jewellery designs!

Felted ball bracelet

This design has been created using the "Making felt balls" technique below. The balls you make can be any size you want. Just keep adding more Filz-it wool tops and diluted detergent to create bigger ball shapes. The number of balls you make will depend on the size of your wrist.

You might also like to use different colours. In my design I've used blue and purple together, but you could try red and pink, for example. Make sure you pick a ribbon that complements your colour choices.

Making felt balls

1. Follow my making felt techniques on pages 20–21 (Steps 1–3). On Step 2 create a small bunch of layers and, using your hands, scrunch up the felted fabric to try and make a small wool bundle. Separate out the wool with your fingers before you wet the fabric.

2. Once the fabric has been sprayed, roll the wool bundle in a fast circular motion using your hands and the bubble wrap. Also cup the wool bundle in your hands and rub it by moving your hand in a circular motion. Keep doing this until you have created a firm ball shape.

Making the bracelet

1. Make the number of balls you need for the length of bracelet you require. To start making your bracelet you will need to thread on your balls using a matching colour of Anchor Alcazar embroidery thread. Pierce the centre of each ball with your needle and embroidery thread.

2. Once you have threaded on all of your balls and beads, sew on a 20cm (8in) piece of ribbon at each end of the bracelet so you can tie it together.

Special tips:

Felting balls can sometimes take a long time to make so you might need to be a little patient but it is always worth it once you get to see the end result. Try to keep squeezing out excess water in Step 2, which will help to make the bundle turn into a ball shape more quickly.

Pretty purse.

This project is so versatile it could be used as a daytime purse, pencil case, make-up bag or even glammed up for a party or disco. Use it as a way of practising some of the basic hand-stitch techniques on pages 14–15. Decorate the purse with running stitches, French knots, beads, sequins or your own felt motifs. If you have already mastered the flower loom, then why not try adding flowers to your purse!

Charlotte says:

In this project I have decorated the purse with butterfly motifs, but you could try something different – why not use the flower loom to make a flower and sew that on? Interesting buttons can make great decorations as well as iron-on sequin motifs and decorative hand stitches.

Making a purse

The great thing about this purse project is that it is simply made from one piece of fabric which is folded three times to make the back, front and flap. If you wish to make a bigger or smaller purse just increase or decrease the size of your base fabric. A simple way to measure your base fabric is to use a piece of A4 paper as a template.

In order to make the purse stronger, so that it isn't floppy, you will need to use felt as the lining fabric. Use Bondaweb to attach the fabric to the felt lining – it will be easier to work with.

To prepare for the project you will need to cut a piece of fabric (for the outside), a piece of felt (for the inside) and a piece of Bondaweb to go in between the two (like the filling in a sandwich). All three of these pieces of fabric need to be identical in size.

Making the purse

1. Peel the paper layer back from the Bondaweb and attach it to the wrong side of the cotton fabric. Then place the remaining fabric piece on top to make a "sandwich".

2. The fabric sandwich needs to be ironed in order to melt the Bondaweb and glue all the layers together. Ask an adult for help if you need it.

3. Use pinking shears to create a zigzag edge on your fabric. Fold the bottom of the fabric upwards to form the purse shape and pin in place. Fold over the excess fabric at the top to make the purse flap.

4. Work blanket stitch to secure each of the side edges together. Blanket stitch is worked so the thread lies along the edge, with the needle inserted at right angles to the edge, under the thread. Repeat at closely spaced intervals.

5. Hand stitch a button of your choice in the middle of the bottom part of the purse.

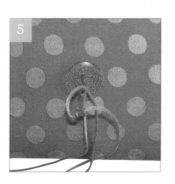

Making the butterfly

6. To make the butterfly motif, place a square of orange felt on top of pink sparkly felt and pin in place. Use a template (page 44) to draw the correct butterfly shape and cut out through both layers of felt.

7. Stitch the butterflies onto the bag flap, adding beads, sequins and French knots for further decoration.

Attaching the ribbon and butterfly

Take your length of ribbon and stitch it to the flap of the purse in the middle. It can then be wrapped around the button and tied in a bow to fasten.

Creating a butterfly template

Use this simple butterfly shape as a template for your purse decoration. Place a piece of tracing paper or thin white paper over the butterfly and trace over the shape. Cut the butterfly shape out with scissors – you now have your very own template which can be used to make the felt butterfly.

Pretty purse alternative

Once you have mastered the method of making a purse you can then begin to play around with different designs. This alternative purse is very pretty and incorporates hand embroidery stitches such as running stitch and French knots (pages 14–15). You can use the patterned fabric as a source of inspiration as well as a guide for stitching.

Adding funky covered buttons to the purse will inject more colour and pattern into the design. These purses are great as gifts – they make a unique birthday present for a friend.

Special tips:

Recycled fabrics would be perfect for this project – old denim jeans would look really cool made into a purse, and they are pretty sturdy too! You could use wool yarns for any decorative stitching on thicker fabric.

Bag charms.

You can use bag charms to add decoration to lots of things, such as handbags, purses, key rings or mobile phones. You and your friends could even make matching ones and start a bag charm trend in your school! I'm also going to show you how to design your very own funky buttons, which are a great way to customize your bag charm designs.

Rachel says:

Preparing your fabric

These bag charms are so easy to make using the basic steps to Crocheting and French knitting. I have used flower designs for mine but you might like to create your own designs and shapes!

Bag charms

Your bag charms can be made from pretty yarn, using crochet or French knitting, in the shape of little flowers. The ones shown here measure roughly 6cm (2in) and 10cm (4in) in diameter, but you can vary the size easily by simply making longer crochet chains or French knitting tubes as appropriate. Follow the steps on French knitting (pages 26-27).

Crochet bag charm

Follow the steps on "Crocheting" (pages 24–25). You will need two different sizes of hooks – the smaller one to create the small flower and the larger one for the other.

1. Make six chains and work a slip stitch into your slip knot. This creates one petal shape. Make another six chains and work another slip stitch into the slip knot. Repeat until you have made seven petal shapes.

2. Using your larger hook, do the same as you did for Step 1 to create a larger flower. You might even like to make two larger flowers.

3. Place the flowers with the small one on top of the larger one. Using a darning needle and the yarn, sew through the middle of the two flowers, from front to back and back to front, a few times.

4. To attach the clip to the flower make a chain of eight crochet chain stitches. Take it through the bag charm fastener and attach it to the back of the flower. Sew a circle of felt onto the back of the flower using matching sewing thread.

French knitted charm

This little pink five-petalled flower was made using Patons knitting yarn, but you can use whatever yarn, ribbon or thread your prefer. The woollier the yarn, the softer-looking the flower.

1. Make a long tube of French knitting. Coil the tube as shown to make five petal shapes and pin them together at the centre.

2. Using a darning needle and some matching yarn, stitch through all the petal shapes and pull tight.

3. To attach it to the clip, make a small plait using three strands of the working yarn. Attach one end to the fastener and one end to the back of the flower.

Decorating your charm

For my bag charms I decided to decorate and customize them using my very own button designs and a Prym button base. Embroidered buttons are a great way to add decoration and you can create your very own button designs by changing the colours of wool you use and selecting different holes to stitch into on the button base.

Embroidered button bases come in two different sizes. Once you have covered your buttons you might like to add beads or sequins to them to give your charms some extra glamour, as I have done with mine.

French knitted charm with plaited string and matching embroidered button.

Crocheted ribbon charm with toning beaded button.

Making embroidered buttons

These embroidered buttons are easy to make using a Prym button base. By using different combinations of colours and types of yarns, as well as beads, and by working different sections on the embroidered button base, you can create a great range of button designs.

Ribbony blue and green big button.

Fancy little pink sparkly button.

Chunky button with bead centre.

Shiny gold and silver big button.

Two-tone button with sparkly centre.

Two-tone button with bead centre.

1. Make sure you have enough yarn/ribbon to work the button or the area you plan to cover. Using a large-eyed needle, take the thread up through the centre of the button. Working from front to back, work around the edge of the button or work in specific sections, depending on the design. Then go through the middle of the button from back to front again.

2. Repeat Step 1 until all of the button (or the chosen section) has been covered.

Picture frames.

Do you have loads of great photographs of your favourite pets, friends, pop stars or family members and aren't sure what to do with them? Then you should have a go at this fab heat transfer and Bondaweb project. It teaches how to use the heat transfer technique to make funky pictures for your bedroom, personalized badges, buttons and even unique greetings cards and invitations!

Charlotte says:

Before starting you will need to choose a favourite photograph and cut a piece of fabric big enough to transfer the image onto. The great thing about transferring an image onto fabric is that you can then sew directly onto it and stitch on beads and sequins without it tearing or ripping.

Picture frames

Decorating a favourite picture can make it extra special. I love to think of creative special effects for my best-loved photographs! This project not only shows you how to decorate a photo with funky fabric shapes but also demonstrates the heat transfer technique. You may have seen this also called T-shirt transfer. Basically it allows you to transfer an image from a photo onto a piece of fabric, T-shirt, cushion cover, fabric badge or whatever you fancy – it's magic!

1. Following the instructions on the packet of heat transfer paper, either photocopy or print a picture directly onto the special paper. Place the heat transfer paper (now with an image of your photograph on it) face down onto your piece of fabric and iron over the back.

2. Peel off the gridded backing paper to reveal the photograph on your piece of fabric – this is now ready to be decorated.

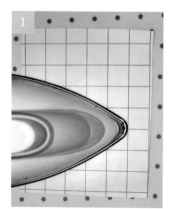

3. From the selection of fabrics and felt that you have available, cut out a variety of shapes, these could be flowers, hearts, cupcakes or whatever goes with your picture. Make sure you have enough shapes to go the whole way around the edge of your picture to make a frame. Place the fabric shapes onto the piece of Bondaweb and use a pencil to draw around each one individually and cut out the shapes.

4. Arrange the shapes around the picture to frame it, making an attractive irregular edge. Take special care to ensure that the relevant Bondaweb layer is underneath each shape, effectively sandwiched between the two fabrics.

5. Iron over the top of the fabric shapes to attach them onto the base fabric.

6. To embellish the photograph, stitch buttons, beads and sequins onto the shapes which frame the picture. Your picture could now be framed in a typical glass frame or it could be attached to a canvas block.

special tips:

You can buy special heat transfer or T-shirt transfer paper from your local stationers. It is usually sold in A4-sized sheets which are perfect for transferring photographs. The special transfer paper will work with your home computer and printer or a photocopier.

Applying the designs to other items

If you would like to adapt and develop the techniques you have just learnt, try making a badge or stitched card. Follow the same instructions to transfer the image onto fabric, stitch into it as desired and attach to a circle of card if you wish to make a badge or apply to a greeting card to make personal party invitations or special cards. This is such a versatile technique – you don't always have to use photographs, drawings and doodles can also look very effective!

Little cosies.

Why don't you have a go at my finger knitted cosy project ideas? These are great things to make to protect your ipod or mobile phone. You will need to work with a friend on these projects as you need eight fingers on which to make them! This is because the cosies you are creating need to be pretty big as you are going to felt and shrink them afterwards in the washing machine.

1 ball of each colour
   of Wash & Filz-it
   (3 cosies per ball)
A friend
Darning needle
Pillowcase
Washing machine
Detergent
Coats Cotton sewing
   thread (to match
   shade of Filz-it
   yarn)

Rachel says:

Before casting off
your stitches and
felting your cosy,
measure your fabric
against your ipod or
mobile phone and
fold it over to see if
it is going to be big
enough. Remember
it will shrink a bit
so at this stage it
should be a little too
big for your ipod or
mobile.

Little cosies

I have used special wool for my cosies called
Wash & Filz-it, which felts really well, but any
pure wool could be used instead. When you
machine wash this wool once it has been
knitted, the fibres in the wool bind together and
you are left with a nice, strong piece of felted
fabric. Follow my simple steps on how to make
your cosy but then try some designs of your
own. The shapes are not perfect because you
are using your fingers and not proper knitting
needles! You can decorate the cosies with
embroidery stitches (pages 14–15) or pompoms,
if you wish (page 63).

Making a plain cosy

1. Using your chosen
yarn, wrap it around
all eight of your friend's
fingers (with little fingers
together and the backs
of their hands facing
you). Then start to finger
knit in the usual way (as
shown on pages 22–23).
You will have cast on
eight stitches and you

need to work at least 35
to 40 rows, depending
on how big you want
your cosy to be. As you
are going to be felting it
afterwards, remember
that it shrinks by about
25 per cent, so make
sure you make enough
rows of knitting.

1

2. When your finger knitting is long enough, cast off as shown on pages 22–23. You will then need to sew up your cosy before you felt it in the washing machine.

3. Fold the fabric over to make a cosy shape and, using a darning needle and some Filz-it wool, sew the sides up.

4. Place your cosy inside a pillowcase, and knot the open end of the pillowcase. Put it into the washing machine and wash it on a 60-degree cycle, to which detergent has been added. Then take it out and leave to dry. You can decorate it if you wish with wool embroidery or pompoms, as shown overleaf.

Making a striped cosy

To make stripy covers, you can add in a new colour where you want to create a stripe. Simply cut the old yarn before starting a new row and lay the new yarn across your friends' fingers. Work it in the same way you have been working with the old yarn. You can darn in the ends of each colour using a darning needle when the fabric has been cast off. You can add in colours randomly or perhaps you could create a repeating pattern by adding in a new colour or colours after every two, four or six rows, and so on.

Customizing your cosy

Once you have made your cosy designs you might like to customize and decorate them like I have – try my different ideas for glamming up your cosies with hand embroidery stitches, felted pompoms or a little crochet chain handle.

You could also add a felted bow, by finger knitting on four fingers, working 10 rows of knitting, folding the knitted fabric over and then sewing the ends of the fabric together using a darning needle and matching wool yarn.Sew through the centre and pull tight to make your final bow shape. Place the bow in the washing machine when you felt the main cosy. Attach it by sewing through the centre a few times until it is secure.

Why not add a wool pompom or two to your cosy design? Make them first (see opposite) and then felt them with the main cosy.

Or you could add a pretty embroidered flower to your cosy using some contrasting wool yarns stitches (see page 15). I've also thread a piece of ribbon through the top of this cosy design using a darning needle so it is like a little pouch.

Or you could make a handle for your cosy by crocheting a chain of matching yarn (see page 25).

Making pompoms

Making pompoms is so quick and easy to do these days as there are lots of good pompom makers around. I have used a Prym pompom maker. In a set you will get four different sizes. Look at the size of the project you are making to see what size would be best to use. You can use any kind of yarn – thick or thin, hairy or soft. You can also use ribbons, fabrics and trimmings. Experiment and try out making lots of different pompoms!

Here's how to create a basic pompom.

3. Using sharp scissors, start cutting in between the gaps of the pompom maker.

1. You should have four plastic half-circles. Place two odd half-circles together and tie a bit of yarn onto them and make a knot. Start wrapping your working yarn around the two half-circles holding them tightly together. Continue this until you think you have enough yarn wrapped around.

2. Now repeat Step 1 for the other two half-circles. If you like, you could do the other side in a different colour of yarn. When complete, click your pompom maker together.

4. Tie a piece of yarn around the gaps and tie tightly. Remove the pompom maker and the pompom should turn into ball. Fluff it up to finish.

More ideas for things to make & do.

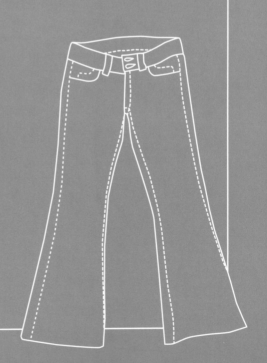

Creating new fabrics

Thanks to new technology today we have lots of brilliant and innovative new materials to use in our textile projects. Soluweb/ Solufleece (known as embroidery stabilizer) are dissolvable material sheets that allow you to make your own sparkly, woven, crazy patchwork and lacy fabrics. The word "soluble" means something that will dissolve (or turn into liquid) when submerged in water.

These new products are fantastic for creating exciting fabric effects. The possibilities are endless!

In this section we are going to show you how to make pieces of fabric from scratch and also how to turn existing clothing fabrics into items such as wall tidies and bags. You will need to use a sewing machine (page 16) and you may need an adult to help you. You can use old scraps of fabrics, threads, sequins and yarns in these projects – so have a rummage through your scrap-bag and see what bits and bobs you can find.

We have created four exciting projects for you to make; a wall tidy, a gorgeous purse, a silky scarf and a pretty felted bag. We also give you lots of hints, tips and samples – the aim here is to explore, experiment and explore some more!

Using soluble fabric

By trapping threads, yarns and wools, fabrics and sequins in between two layers of special soluble fabric you can make your own unique and unusual fabrics, which can then be made into a whole range of different items like scarves, belts, cushions, bags and even bowls and containers.

New fabric from old

Think about using yarns and fabrics that are different colours, thicknesses or textures. Wool can be laid in strips, grids or coiled into circles. Try cutting shapes from various fabrics and arranging them in interesting ways. Use your imagination and see if you can come up with some crazy shapes and patterns!

Work out the size of the piece of fabric you want. Cut two pieces of the special soluble fabric (such as Soluweb) to the required size. Lay one piece of it on the table and begin laying out your lengths of wool, yarn or scraps of fabric on top.

Arranging fabric scraps

Trapping and stitching

Once you have finalized the design you can place the other identical piece of soluble fabric on top, creating a sandwich effect. All the pieces of wool, yarn thread, fabric and sequins will now be trapped between the two layers. Using a sewing machine, make a grid pattern by stitching first vertical and then horizontal lines across the top layer. The stitched lines should be around 1.5cm (2in) apart. If you use a free-motion embroidery foot (see page 17), you could make curved or circular stitched lines. The most important thing to remember is that all the lines MUST connect or overlap, otherwise your fabric will fall apart.

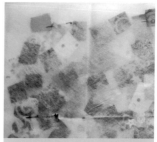
Sandwiching the scraps

Stitching in place

Dissolving

Once the stitching is finished, and all the bits and pieces trapped, place the entire piece of fabric in warm water and rinse until all the gluey stickiness has completely dissolved. The soluble fabric sheets will totally disappear and you will be left with only the stitched areas – yarns, wools and fabrics – that were sandwiched in between. The fabric should feel soft. If any glue is left on the fabric, it will dry hard and stiff. If so, repeat the rinsing process and dry thoroughly.

Dissolving the Soluweb

Creating new fabrics ★ 67

Charlotte's fabric samples

Here are three ideas for hand-made fabrics using dissolving fabric. As you can see, each has a very different character, but I have been careful when choosing the colours to create a "colour palette". In other words, I have concentrated on a limited range of colours in each piece. This will help to make your own design look attractive and "professional". One way to work out a colour palette is to pick a few colours that you like, and then see how the various colours work together on different coloured backgrounds. You could try this on coloured sugar paper to check it out before choosing the fabrics for your design.

Crazy mix

Here I have cut small squares of different printed, plain and spotted fabrics which were then sandwiched in between two sheets of Soluweb and machine stitched in a grid formation. This idea creates a great crazy patchwork effect.

Lilac lace

This shows a technique often called machine lace. You can make your own lace very quickly by simply free-motion stitching onto single pieces of soluble material. Make small, loopy and interlinking stitched circle shapes, dissolve as before and you will be left with a very delicate fabric.

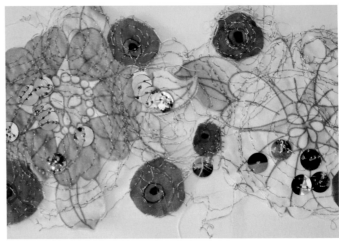

Glitterbug

Sequins or feathers can be sprinkled onto your design before it is sandwiched between the layers of dissolving fabric. The sewing machine can stitch over sequins and feathers without a problem. Remember to take more care when stitching over thicker textured pieces. Sparkly fabrics look great made into purses or handbags.

Charlotte's purse

I have made a little purse using my Crazy Mix fabric. The purse is similar to the one on page 40. I have machine-stitched the sheet of dissolved fabric onto a backing piece of felt to give it extra strength before starting to make the purse. To give some extra detail and sparkle I added a few co-ordinating buttons and sequins, cut a scalloped border on the flap and added a ribbon bow to tie the purse.

Rachel's yarn samples

As well as using fabrics, you can use lots of different yarns and threads to create your own fabrics. You can experiment with different thicknesses and textures; you might also like to finger knit or crochet with the yarn before you apply it to the Soluweb. There are so many ways to create different textures of yarn fabrics. Here are some basic ideas to get you started, with a little project idea opposite to inspire you to make your very own design using this technique.

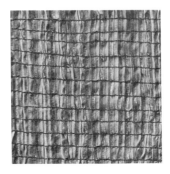

Ribbons galore
Here I used straight pieces of ribbon yarn and laid them vertically onto the Soluweb before machine stitching horizontally across them. This is so simple but can look really effective if you use a fancy type of yarn. You might even like to use different colours of the same yarn and leave bigger spaces between the lines of stitching.

Chunky chains
Here I used a chunky yarn and crocheted with it to make chains, which I then applied to the Soluweb before machine stitching horizontally across them. I used one size of hook but you could use different hook sizes to create different textures. Or you could try crocheting different yarns together.

Mohair mix
For this I used a mohair and acrylic mix yarn and finger knitted with it (pages 22–23) before placing it on the Soluweb. I then machine stitched horizontally across it. I just finger knitted on one finger but you might like to experiment and finger knit on two, three or four fingers before applying it.

Rachel's scarf

I designed and made a scarf to show you what you can actually make with this technique. I used some fancy yarn with which I crocheted long chains and then applied these to the Soluweb. I used shimmery thread on my sewing machine and then stitched horizontally over the chains, leaving quite big gaps. If you follow the simple principles discussed in "New Fabric from Old" on page 67, you could make your own version of this scarf design using whatever yarns and colours you choose.

special tips:

Make sure when cutting your piece of Soluweb fabric that it is going to be long enough for the scarf to wrap around your neck (measure it against a scarf you already have).

Once the scarf is made, glam it up with a fancy pin or brooch design which matches the yarn colours.

Recycling clothes

You have probably heard the word "recycling" before. Recycling means taking an existing object or material that has already been used and then turning it into something else, to make something new from something old.

You can recycle many different things and there are many different ways to recycle.

In this section we are going to show you how to recycle clothes! This is a fun way to create something new without spending too many pennies! To find clothing to recycle you could either visit your local charity shop or simply delve into the wardrobes in your house and find something that isn't worn anymore either by you or one of your family members (make sure you ask them first before you start chopping!).

We are going to get you started by showing you two fun ways of recycling – using denim jeans and old sweaters – and we have each designed a project that you might like to try for each technique. These will hopefully inspire you to create your very own "new from old" designs!

New designs from old

By taking apart and cutting up old denim jeans or skirts you can create fabrics which can be stitched back together and customized to create lots of cool designs. If you machine wash pure-wool sweaters until they felt, you can cut them up so they don't fray and then remodel them into something new and different!

Recycling denim

Jeans are still high fashion which means your family members will be wearing them out on a regular basis. Don't let them go to waste, as, with a little bit of imagination, they can be turned into something fantastic.

Denim is a great hard-wearing fabric which is perfect for many different items, such as bags, jackets, skirts, trousers, pencil cases and lots more! Denim comes in a variety of different colours and thicknesses which is great for making a patchwork effect. To create contrasting designs use light and dark denim together – for example, a bag made from light denim with a dark denim flower or vice versa. Also, make the most of those fab jeans pockets – they have hundreds of uses! I show you how to make a little project overleaf that does just that.

Deconstructing denim
To get the most fabric out of your old jeans or denim jacket, use a special unpicker tool or a small pair of sharp scissors to carefully unpick the stitching along the seam lines.

Stitching denim
Denim is usually thick so make sure you use a sharp needle when stitching or embroidering onto the fabric.

Charlotte's tips:

Customizing your design

You could also customize and embellish your recycled denim design afterwards with buttons, beads, embroidery stitches. Attach other materials using Bondaweb.

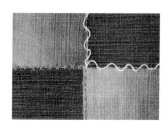

Recycling knitted garments

Sweaters and cardigans are knitted (or crocheted) from many different yarns. But if you try to cut up a knitted garment to turn it into something else it will just unravel at the edges. This does not happen if you felt it first in the washing machine (which effectively makes the knitting shrink and become thicker and more matted). However, you can only felt wool yarns, so check the label to make sure it is at least 80 per cent pure wool and is not machine washable, as some pure wools are treated for machine washing and will not then felt.

Preparation

The best way to felt knitted or crocheted fabrics is to use a washing machine although you can also felt fabric by hand in hot water. Remember that your sweater or cardigan is going to shrink by around 25 per cent so make sure it is big enough for your chosen design. Once the fabric has shrunk and felted, you need to allow it to dry, and then you can cut into it without it falling apart.

Machine felting

You will need to place your jumper inside a pillowcase with a knot tied in it, and then place the pillowcase inside your washing machine along with the detergent. You will need to set your machine to a 60-degree wash cycle. Once your sweater has been washed and felted, take it out and leave it to dry.

Cutting and sewing

Now that your garment has been felted you can cut it into any shape you like. You might like to take the sleeves off or remove the bottom of it and the collar if it has one. Once you have chosen your design, the best way to sew the fabrics together is to use a matching colour of sewing thread unless you want to use an embroidery yarn to blanket stitch the raw edges together (page 43).

Customizing your design

You could also customize your felted fabric with embroidery stitches, buttons, pompoms, knitted flowers, and so on. Or by cutting up any surplus bits of felted fabrics and curling them up to make different shapes.

Rachel says:

Recycling sweaters

Try cutting your jumper or cardigan up in different ways. By doing this you can come up with lots of different accessory designs. You may like to make a handbag, corsage or purse. Your choice of design will depend on the shape of the garment you are felting.

Denim Wall tidy

You can create so many different designs from a pair of jeans or a denim skirt such as handbags, belts, corsages, purses and wristbands. Here is a cool denim wall tidy design to introduce you to recycling denim. You can hang it on the door and use it for pencils or pens or your craft bits and pieces.

You Will need:

Pair of denim jeans
Scissors
Iron-on sequin motifs
Sewing machine
Anchor embroidery
  thread
Needle
Coat hanger

Here's how...

Use a big chunk of the jean-leg fabric as a base. Unpick the seams (page 73). If you use the bottom part of the leg it will already be hemmed and save you some time. Now cut off both large pockets from the back of the jeans as well as the small inner front pocket (these will form the wall-tidy pockets).

Add iron-on motifs, following the manufacturer's instructions, and fix the motifs in place on the denim pockets. Arrange the pockets on the base fabric and pin in place. Machine stitch around the sides and base of each pocket to secure. Remember not to stitch the top side as this will need to be open to allow you to store and tidy away all your bits and pieces. Embellish the wall tidy further by working running stitches (pages 14–15) in interesting curved lines on the base fabric. Hem the top side and attach by hand to a coat hanger.

Now you can hang up the tidy on your wall or door and fill with pens and pencils or even use it as somewhere to store your sewing equipment!

Felted bag

The good thing about felted fabric is that it is really strong and firm, which is perfect for making things such as handbags and purses. Here, a felted cardigan is made into a handbag design. It has felted French knitted handles and a cute little flower as decoration. Remember – you don't have to stick to what we have done. There are various ways you can make a sweater into a handbag by cutting off certain parts of it once felted and using different ways of embellishing and customizing it. Why not try designing one yourself?!

You will need:

Felted cardigan
Scissors
Wash & Filz-it wool and ribbon yarns
Sewing needle
Darning needle
Coats Cotton sewing thread
Anchor Tapisserie Wool
Coats patterned felt

Here's how...

Once your cardigan (or sweater) is felted and cut into the required shape, it can be stitched together using some matching sewing thread. To add extra decoration you could embroider running stitches (pages 14–15) around the edges using a darning needle and some fancy ribbon yarn. Make the handles by French knitting some Wash & Filz-it wool and machine-felt them (pages 27 and 61) before sewing them together to make two circle shapes. A cute little flower made from the felted fabric, with a crocheted ribbon for the stem (page 25) and a funky flowery felt centre, adds a lovely finishing touch.

Charlotte's Workshop

I worked with a group of girls from my local young Embroiderer's Guild during their January and February meetings to create a selection of friendship bracelets. This project provided the group members with an insight into what it's like to be a "textile designer". The girls worked to a design brief, with a select range of fabrics and completed their friendship bracelet within the timescale required. Here's how we worked together!

Charlotte says:

Being a textile designer often means that you have to design something specifically for another person, customer or company. It's very important to make the right choice of design. To do this the client or company will give us a what is called a "design brief" (see opposite).

The workshop group

Here are the girls I worked with in my special Friendship Bracelet workshop. They ranged in age from six to fifteen years old, but they all found the workshop really worthwhile.

The girls (from left to right): Hannah 12, Lauren 11, Ellie 10, Livia 6, Ruth 10, Stephanie 15 and Alana 15.

Session one: the brief

At the beginning of the first session, I presented the girls with a design brief. This outlined exactly what was wanted in the final piece or pieces of work and suggested preferences for particular techniques, colours, size and materials.

In the design brief for this workshop I included some questions to help the girls think about the following:

- Who they were actually making the bracelet for.
- Identifying the needs and wants of their best friends, i.e what colours, shapes, motifs or patterns they may prefer.

I gave them a selection of materials and equipment to work from, and they had to make their own choices of colours, yarns and so on to suit their particular design. You can see the results overleaf.

Friendship bracelet design brief

This design brief is to create a friendship bracelet/bangle for your best friend. It is based on the idea of wrapping a wooden bangle and decorating it, but you need to come up with your own unique design.

To help you start to think creatively, answer the following questions:

1. Does she have any hobbies or interests?

2. What are her favourite colours, patterns and shapes?

3. Do you have any special memories of your friendship that could be represented in the bracelet?

4. What does she look like and what is her fashion style?

Write a list of the sewing, embroidery and craft techniques that you would like to use in your bracelet, such as Suffolk puffs.

Write a list of all the fabrics and materials and equipment you would like to use in your bracelet, i.e flower loom, ribbon, etc.

Session one: designing

Once all the girls had completed a design brief we then, as a group, started to think about what techniques could be used in the project. We decided that the girls would wrap fabric around a wooden bangle to create a quick and solid base onto which they could add decoration. The group spent the rest of the first session experimenting with different techniques and thinking about which ones they would like to incorporate into their own design.

Techniques for decorating the bangle

Wrapping
Felt shapes (such as butterflies, hearts)
Braids
Loopy stitched flowers
Flower loom ribbon flowers (page 30)
Stitched-on buttons, beads, etc.

Each member produced a design drawing with notes to explain their choices: colour, pattern, texture and shape.

Session two: making the bangles

In this session the girls wrapped their bangles and decorated them using the techniques they had learnt in Session One. In Session Two, we only had two hours for making so it was important to have done all the preparation and to have clear design drawings to work from.

1. Prepare your bangle decorations. You could make flowers using the flower loom (page 30) or cut shapes from felt and fabric (page 37).

2. Cut long strips of fabric or ribbon. Wrap the bangle with the strips of fabric, threads and ribbon and glue in place (ask an adult to help).

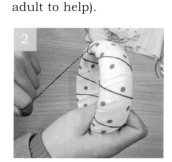

3. Once you have wrapped your bangle with fabric and prepared the decorations, think about where you will place them on the bangle. If you have made heavy flowers or decoration that are too difficult to stitch on you may need to glue these in place.

4. Hand stitch the decorations onto your bangle.

5. Finish off the bracelet by stitching on beads, sequins and charms. These will make your bracelet lovely and sparkly.

Design results

I was very impressed with my group members; they all worked very hard as "textile designers" to make fantastic, colourful bangles to give as gifts to their best friends. Each girl thought carefully about who they were making it for and planned which materials they could use to reflect their friend's characteristics, interests, hobbies or favourite colours. For example, Livia's bangle was very cute; she made it for her friend, Amelia. Livia stitched on two gold snail charms to represent the two African land snails that her friend looks after as pets. On the opposite page are some of the comments that the girls made after the workshop sessions.

Each bangle is individual and unique, and each displays interesting combinations of colour and great use of the techniques learnt in the earlier workshop session. I was especially impressed by how well the girls took on board the "textile design" approach and embraced the idea of working to the design brief.

Although my group had a good knowledge of sewing and embroidery, I think non-sewing groups would enjoy it too, so it would be a great project for Brownies, Guides and other after-school clubs.

"I really enjoyed the workshop with all the techniques that Charlotte has taught me. I made my bangle with the design I gave it because I like spots and so does Stacey and she wears a lot of pink flowery clothes."

Ruth

"I learned how to use a flower loom to make different-sized flowers and the best part was actually assembling the bracelet together. It was lots of fun and I'd love to do it again!"

Stephanie

"I really enjoyed making the bracelet because I like working hard to make one thing but I actually tried a lot of new things. I made my bracelet for my friend Rachel. Rachel likes horse riding and that gave me the idea of a horse-head charm."

Ellie

Rachel's Workshop

My workshop took a bit longer than Charlotte's and involved four separate sessions. I worked with six girls from my local primary school over a two-week period (for a day per session).

I asked them to work in two groups: each had to create their own collection of accessories using the techniques I have used in the book, with the idea of selling them at a craft fair.

So as a result of our four sessions, the girls learned not only how to design, but how to work together to create a specific result. As you will see from their comments, they learned a lot!

Rachel says:

I divided the workshop into four sessions to create a structure:

1. Introducing the task and teaching craft techniques.
2. Research, inspiration and drawing.
3. Designing and making labels.
4. Finalizing designs and selling them.

The workshop group...

Here are the girls I worked with in my special accessory designing workshop. The youngest was aged 10 and the oldest was aged 11.

The girls (from left to right): Claire, Frances Anne, Rebecca, Anna, Emily and Rachel.

Session one: preparation

At the first session I presented the six girls with their group task and the deadline for it. I then introduced the girls to some basic craft techniques that they would employ in the later sessions to make their chosen designs, for example how to felt (pages 20–21), how to French knit (pages 26–27), how to crochet (pages 24–25), how to embroider buttons (page 51), how to make pompoms (page 63) and how to work hand embroidery stitches (pages 14–15).

The group design brief

Your task is to work in your group to produce a collection of accessories using the techniques from the workshops. Once you have completed your designs you will make professional labels for your collection. You will then hold a small craft fair in your school to sell your creations.

Group A: Design a collection of hair accessories (hair bands, slides/clasps, bobbles).

Group B: Design a collection of brooches.

"I enjoyed French knitting the most, I was so excited at the start of the lesson. I am really looking forward to doing the actual designing part in our groups, I hope my group has good ideas."

Claire

"I learned how to crochet and felt, I really like crochet but I don't really like felting."

Frances Anne

"We did felting, crochet and made buttons today. I liked crocheting the best because it is really easy, quick to do and good fun!"

Rebecca

"I liked being able to choose the different types of wools from the shade charts, that was so much fun, it felt like you were a proper designer!"

Claire

"I really enjoyed helping Emily and Frances with the colour palettes…"

Rachel

Session two: sketches and designs

At the second session the girls were split into their groups. I asked them first of all to make decisions on the techniques they would like to you use, their market and their colour palette. Group A decided on a warm colour palette – reds, pinks and purples – and Group B decided on a cool colour palette – blues, creams and greens. The girls also looked through magazines and books, and at my own designs, to find some inspiration for theirs.

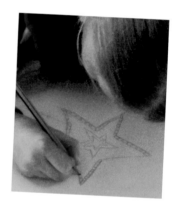

In the second half of this session I asked the girls to work individually and produce some sketches and design ideas. After doing this they came back together as a group and we decided whose ideas would work best. Finally they picked out which products they would like to use to make their final collections.

Session three: presenting designs

At this session the girls began designing and making some samples, experimenting with the techniques they had learned. I gave them A1 presentation boards and got them to the stick down some of their samples and design ideas and their chosen label for their collection. Group A came up with "Peekabow" and Group B came up with "Stardom". They came up with these label names based on their design ideas. Group B also ended up making their own sketchpads to record their ideas in.

I then got each group to present their ideas to me and talk about how they were going to create their final design collection. We then made decisions together about materials, design ideas and so on, and then the girls went off to make a start on their final collection.

"I really liked doing the presentation boards because there was so much you could do with it. You could stick buttons on it, beads, clips, felt and paper. You could also colour things in too. This has been my favourite day so far!"

Rachel

The group's label designs

Here are the two labels that each group came up with and their comments about them.

Group A · Peekabow

"We decided to call our label 'Peek-a-bow'. It was really exciting coming up with a name, you felt like you were a professional designer"

Emily

"Our design label is called 'Stardom'. I really liked coming up with the name with my group."

Rebecca

Group B · stardom

Session four: design results

I was so proud of my girls, they worked really hard during this project and I was very impressed with their end results! They seemed to really enjoy the workshops, especially learning the new techniques, and working together in their groups seem to give them confidence to be able to make decisions and be creative.

Group A . peekabow

They liked finger knitting, embroidering buttons, hand embroidery and pompom making the best. They made the bow designs from different colours of Coats felt which they embroidered around using Patons yarn, Prym embroidered buttons for the centres, and pompoms. They decided to design and make their hair bobbles using French knitting and for their hair bands they used a basic hair band wrapped around with yarn.

Group B . stardom

They liked crochet, felting and hand embroidery the best. They used Anchor Filz-it felt they had created for their star base; they then cut out star shapes from felt and sewed them onto their designs. For two of the designs the girls used pinking shears to cut out star shapes and they also used some hand embroidery techniques on one of the brooches. The middle of the star was created using crochet chains, rolled into circles and embellished with beads. They plaited and made crochet chains for the bits of fabric hanging down from the stars and attached hand-felted bobbles on the end of them.

The girls then decided on prices for their designs and we set up a mini craft fair at lunch time and they sold some of their creations.

Group A . Peekabow

"On day 1 I really didn't like felting but now I do, it's just that on the other day my piece of felt was quite bad, but now my felt is good because Emily helped me and now I can show people how it's done."

Frances Anne

"I liked working with Rachel and Frances Anne and coming up with ideas together. I like doing felting the most in this project because it was so easy and fast to do and I have never done anything like that before, I hope I do more."

Emily

"I have wanted to be a designer for such a long time and this has made me want to be one even more, I have loved it...to be a designer you don't have to just design clothes and things, you can design anything really...I loved designing brooches they were really fun to make!"

Rebecca

Group B . stardom

It is always
best to stick
to small
projects when
organizing a craft
fair. If your projects
are small they will
be quicker to make,
therefore you will be
able to create more
stock and sell it at a
nice little price.
We suggest the
following: Corsages/
brooches, jewellery
(friendship bracelets,
necklaces, rings,
etc.), cards, purses,
mobile/ipod cosies,
bag charms and
key rings.

If your fair is
successful you and
your friends might
even want to start
your very own craft
business in your
school, perhaps you
could hold a
monthly fair and
keep making and
selling your
creations.

setting up a craft fair

Setting up a craft fair either in your school,
club or local community centre is a good way to
sell things that you and your friends have made
and a great way to show off your designs to all
your other friends, teachers and parents. Follow
our simple steps opposite on how to set up your
very own craft fair and make it work! Ask your
parents to help organize the venue.

A month before...

1. Come up with a date for your craft fair and book your venue. (school assembly hall, gym, library, canteen or reception?).

2. Work with your friends to produce posters advertising the craft fair and stick them up in your school.

3. Decide with your friends what type of things you would like to sell and decide who is going to make what.

4. Start working on your stock for your fair, this could perhaps be done on your morning or lunch break or after school with your friends.

A week before...

5. Once your designs are completed, make some lovely labels and tags for them.

6. Make a price list for all the things you will be selling.

7. Find a nice table to display your work and think about how you will display it – presentation is the key!

The day before...

8. Start sticking up large bold and colourful posters saying "Craft fair this way!" with arrows pointing in the direction.

The morning of the fair...

9. Get all set up and delegate two people to be in charge of taking the money.

It's action time..!

10. Put a big smile on your face and tell people how you made all your lovely creations, model them on each other and get other people to try them on and fingers crossed you will have some pennies coming your way!!!

setting up a stitch club

Setting up a stitch club is a fantastic way to meet new people, make new friends and learn new skills at the same time. There are loads of places you can set up your group but it is probably best to keep it fairly small to begin with so you can meet in your own houses until you have got it going. Then you can invite more friends and, with an adult to help, you can move to a local hall or community group. If you follow our top ten tips opposite, you will have covered the basic steps, and you will then be ready to go!

Charlotte & Rachel say:

We have managed to set up our own stitch clubs where we live so you can too, it is so easy peasy! Just follow our simple steps shown opposite!

The basic steps

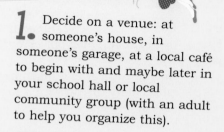

1. Decide on a venue: at someone's house, in someone's garage, at a local café to begin with and maybe later in your school hall or local community group (with an adult to help you organize this).

2. Decide on a time you want to meet at, how long you want to meet for and how often you would like to hold it. You could run it one day a week or you might like to just run it once a month.

3. Decide on a cool name for your stitch club. Here's some of our suggestions: "The Stitch Divas", "The Stitching Girls", "Stitch It", "Our Stitching Circle", "Stitch and Chat", "Crafts and Cakes".

4. Make some flyers to advertise your stitch club. We suggest making your own hand-made flyers or cards and send or hand out these to people you think might like to come along. You might also ask your school if you can put a poster or flyer up in the school.

5. Remember not to worry if you don't have a lot of people interested at first, three is enough to begin with. You will find that more will join as time goes on!

6. Ask your mums, dads, aunties, uncles, grandparents for any equipment, materials, books they might like to donate to your stitch club. Charity shops are great places to find stitching equipment!

7. Each week ask your group to bring along anything they have made to help inspire the other members of the group.

8. Remember – all that stitching gives you an appetite! Why not each take a turn to bake cakes to take along to the club?

9. Invite art and craft teachers or creative parents along every so often to your stitch club and get them to pass on some new skills to you and your group or teach them something!

10. Finally, write to local newspapers and magazines to try and get a feature about your stitch club. This will inspire other school girls to start one up and before you know it you will have a whole network of stitch clubs in your area!

suppliers & products

The yarns, threads and haberdashery used in this book are all supplied by Coats Crafts UK. Their main address is listed below. More detailed lists of stockists can be found on their website.

Coats Crafts UK
Lingfield Point
McMullen Road
Darlington, Co. Durham
DL1 1YJ
www.coatscrafts.co.uk
tel +44(0)1325 394237

Yarns and threads
Patons yarns come in several weights, types and colours. Diploma Gold DK yarn is an all-purpose wool blend machine-washable yarn.

Anchor Wash & Filz-it is a 100 per cent wool yarn that is ideal for felting, as it felts when washed at 60 degrees.

Anchor Filz-it wool tops are designed for wet felting and needle felting.

Anchor Tapisserie Wool is a 100 per cent wool yarn that can be used for embroidery or for knitting or crocheting small items.

Coats Cotton sewing thread is for machine and hand stitching, ideal for cotton fabrics.

Coats Duet sewing thread is for machine stitching polyester fabrics.

Anchor Alcazar is a machine embroidery thread with a lustrous sheen.

Fabrics
Anchor Style & Filz-it felt is available in A4 sheets in various styles: plain, glitter, patterned and embossed, in a wide range of colours.

Haberdashery and equipment
Prym iron-on rhinestones are available in a range of designs and letters.

Prym French knitting dollies are available in two sizes, small and large.

Index

Acknowledgements

This book has been lots and lots of fun to do and very very exciting! Everyone has worked so hard on it, especially our publisher and editor Susan Berry who made this all happen and whom we would like to thank loads, as well as Ama and Nicky our book designers who have made "Stitch Divas" so sparkly and just lovely! And, of course, all of our gorgeous Stitch Diva girls for taking part!

Most importantly we would like to thank Sharon Brant for suggesting that we work together on such a project in the first place and being a constant support to us both. And let's not forget an extra big thanks to Coats Crafts for giving it all the go ahead!

From Charlotte...

It's been an absolute pleasure to work with you Rachel. I've really enjoyed sharing ideas and techniques with you and learnt so much more about knitting, felting and crochet. It's been fab to work with someone so like minded, a huge thank you for making it so fun!

I would like to say thank you to the girls at Darlington Young Embroiderers Guild who were fantastic to work with. I'm sure you all agree – your friendship bangles look amazing!!!

A big thank you goes to my family and friends for constant support. And to my lovely doggy Alfie (I know you can't read this), but thank you for being such a good model and for letting me make you look quite girlie in the picture frame project!

My final thanks goes to Michelle for creating the wonderful fairy illustrations of Rachel and I, I absolutely love them! Thanks for all your hard work, effort and enthusiasm this year. It's much appreciated!

From Rachel...

I would first of all like to say a big thank you to my new stitching buddy Charlotte, for being so much fun to work with! You have really inspired me with all great ideas and gorgeous designs!

Second of all I would like to say a big thanks to all my crafty, arty, stichin friends who continue to inspire me throughout my creative journey and just generally make me giggle! – Kate, Amy, Suzie, Kirsty, Jenny, Susan, Alison, Hels, Hils, Jude, Ange and the rest....! I would also like to thank all the lovely, lovely children and teenagers I have met over the years who have also inspired me lots at the following schools: Gylemuir Primary School, The Edinburgh Academy Junior School, Westburn Primary, Beath High School, Dunfermline High School and Grays School of Art – you know who you are!